INDIGENOUS BIOGRAPHIES

Charles Albert Bender

Baseball Star

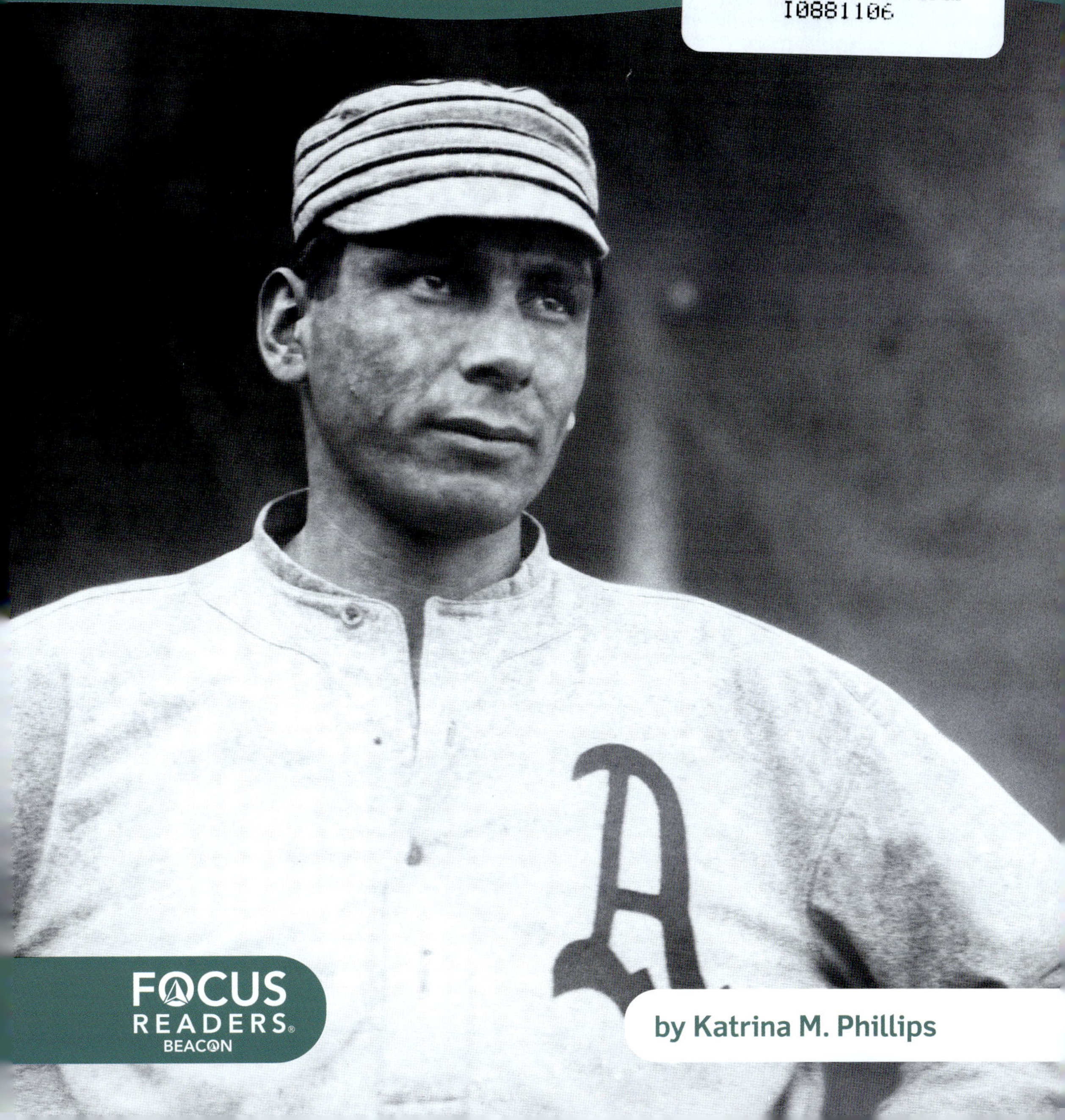

FOCUS READERS BEACON

by Katrina M. Phillips

www.focusreaders.com

Focus Readers is distributed by North Star Editions:
sales@northstareditions.com | 888-417-0195

Produced for Focus Readers by Red Line Editorial.

Photographs ©: Bain News Service/Library of Congress, cover, 1; Joe Vella/Alamy, 4; Paul Thompson/Library of Congress, 6; Shutterstock Images, 8; Jim Mone/AP Images, 11; Library of Congress, 13; John N. Choate/Beinecke Rare Book & Manuscript Library/Yale University, 15; George Rinhart/Corbis Historical/Getty Images, 16; Transcendental Graphics/Archive Photos/Getty Images, 18, 21; AP Images, 22, 24, 27, 29

Library of Congress Cataloging-in-Publication Data
Names: Phillips, Katrina M. author
Title: Charles Albert Bender: baseball star / by Katrina M. Phillips.
Description: Mendota Heights, MN: Focus Readers Beacon, [2026] | Series: Indigenous biographies | Includes bibliographical references and index. | Audience: Grades 2-3
Identifiers: LCCN 2025012043 (print) | LCCN 2025012044 (ebook) | ISBN 9798889984986 hardcover | ISBN 9798889986522 paperback | ISBN 9798889985617 ebook pdf | ISBN 9798889985303 hosted ebook
Subjects: LCSH: Bender, Charles Albert, 1884-1954--Juvenile literature | Ojibwa Indians--Biography--Juvenile literature | Indian baseball players--Biography--Juvenile literature | LCGFT: Biographies | Literature.
Classification: LCC E99.C6 P5233 2026 (print) | LCC E99.C6 (ebook) | DDC 977.004/973330092 [B]--dc23/eng/20250416
LC record available at https://lccn.loc.gov/2025012043
LC ebook record available at https://lccn.loc.gov/2025012044

Printed in the United States of America
Mankato, MN
012026

About the Author

Dr. Katrina M. Phillips (Red Cliff Ojibwe) is a writer, researcher, and history professor. She's written several children's books about Native histories and cultures, including *Indigenous Peoples' Day* and *I Am on Indigenous Land*. She and her husband live in Minnesota with their two sons and their goofy dog.

Table of Contents

CHAPTER 1

World Series Showdown

It was Game 6 of the 1911 World Series. The Philadelphia Athletics faced the New York Giants. The A's led the series three games to two. But the Giants had their star pitcher on the mound.

A huge crowd gathers for Game 6 of the 1911 World Series.

In 1911, Charles Albert Bender had a .773 winning percentage, which led the American League (AL).

The A's manager turned to one of his best pitchers. Charles Albert Bender had already pitched in Games 1 and 4. If he could deliver a win in Game 6, the A's would win the series.

Bender pitched all nine innings. He gave up only two runs. The A's easily won the game.

Bender had pitched 26 innings in the series. He struck out 20 batters. And now he was a champion!

Did You Know?

Bender is credited with inventing the slider. This pitch moves sideways as it goes toward the batter.

CHAPTER 2

From White Earth to Carlisle

Charles Albert Bender was born in Crow Wing County, Minnesota, in 1884. His father was a German **lumberjack**. His Ojibwe mother cooked for the lumberjacks. Charles had 10 siblings.

Charles Albert Bender was born near Partridge Lake in Minnesota.

His family moved when Charles was about four years old. They went to the White Earth **Reservation**. They started a farm there.

Everyone had a job on the farm. Charles's job was to throw rocks out of the fields so the plows wouldn't break. Sometimes he threw the rocks at gophers. He later said this was what gave him such a good pitching arm.

Some Native children went to school on the reservation. Others

Today, there are more than 19,000 citizens of White Earth. Many on the reservation harvest wild rice.

went to **boarding schools** far away from their homes. At seven years old, Charles and two of his siblings were sent to a boarding school. It was called the Lincoln Institution.

The school was near Philadelphia, Pennsylvania. It was more than 1,000 miles (1,600 km) away from Minnesota.

Charles went back to Minnesota when he was 12. But he was not home for long. A few months later, he went to another boarding school.

Did You Know?

There were more than 500 boarding schools in the United States in the 1800s and 1900s.

At Carlisle, Native students were not allowed to wear their traditional clothing.

It was known as the Carlisle Indian Industrial School. It was in Carlisle, Pennsylvania. Charles started at Carlisle in 1896.

TOPIC SPOTLIGHT

Federal Indian Boarding Schools

Carlisle was the first **federal** boarding school that targeted Native children. Nearly 8,000 children were sent to Carlisle over the years. Many more boarding schools opened after Carlisle.

Native students were taken from their families and sent to these schools. Their hair was cut. This aimed to erase their **cultures**. Kids were also not allowed to keep their names. They were punished for speaking their own languages. They could not practice their cultures. Many students died from diseases.

Carlisle often took "before and after" photos of students.
These schools wanted to erase Native cultures.

CHAPTER 3

The Major Leagues

Charles Albert Bender started playing baseball at Carlisle. Charles usually pitched or played second base. He played his first professional game in 1901.

Charles Albert Bender realized how much he loved playing baseball.

Bender (top right) appears with the Philadelphia Athletics in 1905.

Charles's team didn't win that game. But he played well.

As a result, Charles started getting noticed by baseball **scouts**. He signed with the Philadelphia

Athletics. He played his first game with them in 1903. He was only 18 years old. But he was already playing in Major League Baseball (MLB).

Bender pitched well in his first season. His earned run average (ERA) was 3.07. Even so, he still had a lot to learn.

Did You Know?

Charles Albert Bender played in 459 games in his MLB career.

Bender's game improved in 1905. He also reached his first World Series. The A's lost to the Giants. But Bender pitched the only game they won.

Bender and other Native athletes often faced **racism** throughout their careers. Newspaper writers called him "Chief Bender." Bender did not like this nickname. But he tried to avoid showing it when he played.

Bender focused on baseball. He studied other players. He threw new

Bender went 212–127 as an MLB pitcher. He threw 40 shutouts.

pitches to fool batters. By 1910, his ERA was 1.58. It had gone down for eight straight seasons. The A's won their first World Series that year. Bender helped lead them to two more titles in the next three years.

CHAPTER 4

Life After Baseball

Charles Albert Bender stopped playing after the 1917 season. He worked in a **shipyard** at the end of World War I (1914–1918). But he never left baseball. He worked as a scout and a pitching coach.

After retiring, Charles Albert Bender came back to play in a few games.

As a coach, Bender helped MLB pitchers learn to be calm, patient, and in control.

Bender may not have been a professional pitcher anymore. But he still helped make teams better. He helped the A's pitchers lower their ERAs. He also threw in batting practice for the A's until he was in his 60s. At one point, he was the oldest batting practice pitcher in the major leagues.

Bender managed eight minor league teams over the years. He also coached the US Naval Academy's baseball team for six years.

Did You Know?

Bender liked to paint and garden. He also loved to fish, hunt, and play golf.

In 1953, Bender was elected to the Baseball Hall of Fame. He became the first **Indigenous** player to earn that honor.

But Bender did not live to see the ceremony in August 1954. He died on May 22, 1954. He was 70 years old. He had been sick for a long time.

Charles Albert Bender was a World Series-winning pitcher. He was a dedicated coach, and he helped find future professional

Bender was Minnesota's first Baseball Hall of Famer.

players. The boy from Minnesota had gone from boarding schools to the big leagues.

Focus Questions

Write your answers on a separate piece of paper.

1. Write a letter to a friend explaining what you learned about boarding schools.
2. What most impressed you about Charles Albert Bender's career? Why?
3. What pitch is Bender credited with inventing?
    - **A.** fastball
    - **B.** slider
    - **C.** changeup
4. When did Bender join the major leagues?
    - **A.** 1898
    - **B.** 1903
    - **C.** 1917

5. What does **signed** mean in this book?

*He **signed** with the Philadelphia Athletics. He played his first game with them in 1903.*

A. joined a team
B. left a sport
C. changed states

6. What does **elected** mean in this book?

*In 1953, Bender was **elected** to the Baseball Hall of Fame. He became the first Indigenous player to earn that honor.*

A. kicked out of
B. chosen to be part of
C. reminded of

Answer key on page 32.

Glossary

boarding schools
Places where Native children were forced to learn English and forget their cultures.

cultures
The customs, arts, beliefs, and laws of groups of people.

federal
Owned or run by the top level of the US government.

Indigenous
Native to a region, or belonging to ancestors who lived in a region before colonists arrived.

lumberjack
A person who cuts down trees, cuts them into logs, and transports them to a sawmill.

racism
Hatred or mistreatment of people because of their skin color or ethnicity.

reservation
Land set aside by the US government for a Native nation.

scouts
People whose jobs involve looking for talented young players.

shipyard
A place where ships are built and fixed.

To Learn More

BOOKS

Burrell, Dean. *Baseball Biographies for Kids: Stories of Baseball's Most Inspiring Players.* Callisto Kids, 2024.

Ferris, Kade. *Charles Albert Bender: National Baseball Hall of Fame Pitcher.* Lerner Publications, 2026.

Sorell, Traci. *Contenders: Two Native Baseball Players, One World Series.* Penguin Random House, 2023.

NOTE TO EDUCATORS

Visit **www.focusreaders.com** to find links and resources related to this title.

Index

Answer Key: 1. Answers will vary; 2. Answers will vary; 3. B; 4. B; 5. A; 6. B